Dedicated

to Sissy, Joe, Shonna, Cody, and Shannan—
for the feathers

and Margaret Mangahas (Mom)—
for the talons

Pocketing Feathers

Poems by
~~J.D. Isip~~

04/20/2016

Quinces —
Keep every feather
you find — it has
been awesome seeing

you grow

SADIE
GIRL
PRESS

ISBN-13: 978-0692522530
ISBN-10: 0692522530
Copyright 2015 J.D. Isip
Published by Sadie Girl Press

In *Pocketing Feathers*, J.D. Isip takes an elegance I can only say is equaled by Whitman and created a complete photo album of his life in, sometimes, Bukowski-esque bare-knuckle terms. His ideas are complete and the music his words create when read aloud is its own, multi-genre soundtrack. I am amazed at the heart of light even in his most painful memories. Isip does not pull punches. He does not write for shock value. The last thing this gentleman is looking for is pity. No, *Pocketing Feathers* is an honest look into a tumultuous life where self-discovery has its own, unique jazz and growing pains.

—Clifford Brooks, Pulitzer-nominated author of *The Draw of Broken Eyes & Whirling Metaphysics*

Table of Contents

Introduction...v

Frame by Frame **1**

Pitfalls...3

Buttercream 4

The Home 6

Jingle Bells & Jazz...8

Like Her 9

Projects Prayer 10

How to Cook with Government Cheese 11

The Wonderful... 12

Son of a Bitch.. 13

There Are Times 14

Comadre 15

Faraway Words on Jars...................................... 16

Filipino Food.. 17

Sons of Thunder... 18

Passing.. 19

We Were the Tide... 20

Something Significant.. 22

Chow Hall 23

Aviano, 1996.. 24

Windmills 25

Taking It In 27

If We Were Reasonable...................................... 28

Rijksmuseum, 2012 29

The Thing That Is Dragged **31**

The Vertical View of History Holds 33

Exit, Cherry Avenue.. 34

Blackface 35

I Would 36

Deluge 37

In the Ball Crawl 38

How to Be (I) 40

How to Be (II) 41

How to Be (III) 42

How to Be (IV) 43

Dumbo the Flying Elephant 44

Contiguous We 45

Wonderland 46

On the Dance Floor 48

"You Gonna Be Up All Night" 52

One Whole Voice That Is You 53

Hundreds of Smaller Deaths 55

Mamertinum: Sheol 57

Mamertinum: Barnabas 60

Mamertinum: Silas 63

Mamertinum: Rhizome 66

Mamertinum: Timothy 68

Mamertinum: Aftermath 70

Stars 73

The Look into the Canyon 79

The Far Reaches of What Humans Can Find 81

The Mother 82

Estella 83

Business Trip, San Antonio 84

Promotion 85

Soup or Salad 86

Remains 87

Listening 88

Fragmentia 89

Via Negativa 90

Pentecost 91

The Scientist 92
To Grow... 93
The Parable of the Tiger.. 94
This Life More Sweet... 97

Acknowledgements 99
Gratitude... 100
About the Author... 101
About the Cover Art... 102
Notes for "Hundreds of Smaller Deaths" 103

Introduction

Come in. You are welcome here.

You are welcome because you too face loss and anguish, you too must navigate the misplaced yet inevitable presence of irony, you too experience crises of identity and prejudice.

Listen to the voices that ring through these poems. They speak with compassion and awareness. They have learned to continue with grace. Stand beside the speaker who witnesses the aging and dying of a parent. Small moments of humor emerge. We know what the end will bring, but we are led to understand the importance of life, of continuance, of glimmers of joy.

Explore the complications of love—the twists and turns of love within families, the betrayals and acceptances between lovers, and the gestures that widen the divides and bridge the distances when one person opens toward and closes off from another.

Scrutinize the sharp dynamics of poverty that turn on pride and need. Filtered through the promises of family and lovers, see how close pride and need are to the dynamics of desire.

Watch these poems prove eruptive and caustic to the gentle, who despite the corrosion, continue to hold the poisoned—mother, lover, brother—as well as they can, because they must, because "after all this time hell still tried to imitate/heaven."

Delve into the tangled bloodlines of the heart, the ones that cause paralysis when tampered with, that cut off circulation when traced, heroically, for understanding. Even though such "heroism is exhausting," the people here find ways to endure.

Join this family: Hayden, Dickinson, Eliot, Auden, Whitman, and Ginsberg. Watch as this family takes shape and proves as complicated as the bloodlines of all the families gathered here. No mother, father, sister, or brother is presented without scrutiny. No writer could prove great without such studied examination.

Go ahead, "tell them the languages of dreams," remind them that love is work, that transforming hate to love is work, that living is work, and know: There is no better life than the gift of a life devoted to this work.

Thank you, JD, for doing this work.

—**Irena Praitis** author of *Straws and Shadows, One Woman's Life*, and *Branches*

Frame by Frame

the boy turned the square eyes of the old Viewmaster
toward the light that spilled in from the kitchen.
He watched the story figured frame by frame

Shane Seely, "Viewmaster"

Pitfalls

Thinking there was more time, waiting
out an evening or forty, supplicating words
stillborn and scattered in that stone gray
sunrise that settles nothing, promises

only a new monochrome world risen
like ash from ash, she'd say *Let me die, let me*
to every pair of passing feet, every chair
or tottering walker that brushed past

in shadows where her still small voice
joined the chorus from door to door, *Let me*
echoing through unexplored corners
and darkened doorways, every one open

haunted with yellowing eyes, gaping mouths
sending prayer and plea *Let me die, let me*
from the dank, urine-tinged recesses
the nurses avoid or jump past, relieved.

Buttercream

after she had worked her way through the Avon catalogue –
each of us acquiring a dozen flavored lip gloss tubes,
bottles of bubble gum bubble bath, scented candles
we'd light up over the sink (just in case)
black cherry kissing our hands
losing ourselves when it was okay –
she took a Wilton's class downtown on cakes

cross shaped and rabbit shaped and Easter egg oval
silver pans with convenient holes inviting the purchaser
to display them like trophies of culinary feats
artistic prowess never reached
in their splendid, dust-covered perfection
all gathered in enormous bags, put on layaway
to dream of being useful and providing

she flipped through photo albums
at the panadería – birthday cakes with plastic Smurfs,
tiny babies and storks, Mickey Mouse with off colors,
wedding cakes trying to outdo one another
like the dresses in the shop nextdoor
where Sylvia, the seamstress, told her
she looked like she could sew

she believed she could... or would
and poured herself, and, sometimes, the entire
check from Welfare, into the towers
of garish white cakes that climbed and climbed
to the PVC couples that always outlasted
some sailor who bought us ice cream
but never promised to do it again

one stick of soft butter, sugar, a little milk, mix
whatever flavor that fits, whatever color is left
my arm mimicking hers – the luxury of a mixer

I can afford now, but I like the motion
circles I can control
fist tight and sure, around and around
sweetness to cover any damn thing you please

The Home

"That's Agnes," my mother says, as I roll
the wheelchair down the Home's hall, me pushing,
and the sorrowful wails from Agnes pressing
behind us.

"Jesus, make my bowels move! Jesus, make my bowels move!"
I smile and my mother smiles, a little, and we roll
past the floral print wallpaper imitating
the gardens some would tend when they could
tend a garden or defecate
without a prayer.

We make it to the activity room – pokeno in progress –
"The thrill of POKER and the suspense of KENO"
My mother tells me she's good at the game when a nurse
asks her if she needs to use the restroom before it starts
and my mother says no and looks at me, smiles, a little
and says, "You can still hear her, huh?"

I could. The supplications were steady and crushing
like the Home, the drab wallpaper flowers, and my mother fading
into too much rouge, too little lipstick, grey eyes
and questions she asked just moments ago,
"Yeah, mom – Jesus make my bowels move!"

She laughs, so I do. I kiss her goodbye
trying to remember if poker *was* thrilling
or keno held *any* suspense, realizing
I couldn't remember either game,
but I was sure I had played...

"Jesus..." Agnes started as I walked past her room –
I moved too fast through the exit to hear the rest.
She died the next week, when pokeno
was over and my mother was asking me the same question
again, "What did you plant this week, son?"

Jingle Bells & Jazz

I looked again –
Remembering how important everything once was.
Jason Shinder

We only have a few of those ornaments
left over from those days with Ella's
voice as cozy as the champurrado
stirred into a smooth silk sheen by mom
her small legs nudged by a hungry cat

Velvet reindeer, scarlet with black painted
antlers and hooves like the middle keys
on pianos, retro beautiful and too much –
contrapuntal as cold and Christmas,
as Chet Baker and sweet tamales

A little wooden bird, bright orange
with blue and yellow flowers, dots and swirls
in the style of the pottery of Baja
where we watched La Bufadora blow
crazy, all over the place like Parker

Two flat fish, woven out of pink ribbons
given to us by those giggling girls
from the Korean Church we went to
one Christmas Eve to hear *What Child Is This*
Guaraldi-style by a tiny boy in a tuxedo

And the hollow snow man, my favorite
cocky, half-chipped Jelly Roll smile
and a red gloved hand tipping his top hat
as if to say, "Lovely arpeggios, today!"
Because he only speaks jazz.

Like Her

Thirty-eight, maybe forty boxes—
how does that divide by nine marriages?
Old photo albums we don't look through
stacked sideways, shut for years—
A hat box her third husband gave her
from Italy—where she said he died
At least to her—stuffed with Christmas cards
the old 70's, foil kind—flimsy
And showy, now frail, like her

I've begged her to dump them, dump them all
but she protests, she pulls some trick—
A yellowed picture of my dad in a fading, brown suit
or my brother's first card from his father (not mine)—
I digress. To me, it's a waste
like being married nine times
To hold onto the crumbling pieces of a past
that rots away in a rented storage space
Each box as empty as they are full

Married nine times—unfathomable
as these old boxes, stuffed, overflowing
Contents far too daunting, too consuming to explore—
probably not enough to learn from, or care for
To me, it's a waste—I'm not like her—
I'd throw them away
Clean up and move on.

Projects Prayer

She never seemed to sleep:
mornings she wore the green oil factory shirt,
nights the blue smock with Sav-On on a patch,
all day a troubled look, like the hunted
who pause for a breath and prop up their ears
and plot in seconds their next ten moves...

"Say your prayers" and we listened
though we prayed for our father and he never came
and we prayed for more food and a home
and God seemed always too busy to hear
but we prayed, because, well, that's what you do
to ward off the Hate..

The Hate is what made Danny Boy start taking crystal
and his sister started sleeping around, to make a few bucks
and It is the only meal you are sure to get here
in the Projects, and maybe the missionary food
that comes every few months, when the last batch of poor people
wise up and stop praying... and they need more offerings.

"Say your prayers" and I did:
I said, "God, you bastard,
Bless my brother, that he might stop drinking for one night,
Bless my father that he might come back to us,
Bless my sister that she will not be ashamed of us,
Bless my mother that she might not wake up to your lie,
Bless You when you answer to *me*."

She never seemed to sleep:
Mornings she watched me eat the Hate
Nights she watched the Hate eat me
all day, a troubled look...

How to Cook with Government Cheese

It's far too salty to eat right out. You have to let it set. Perhaps until you are not poor. Until your mother has died and the memory of the welfare check and all of it has faded. Has, as the middle class friends you have now might say, mellowed. After some years, there is mold of course. The green stuff that comes from all of the times you hated people for having new clothes and warm food and Christmases. People you never met. People on television screens in cheap motels that kept you for a week or two after the first and the fifteenth of each month. In any case, you can still use it. In fact, you will be surprised how resilient it has been. Decades and it is still sharp. It can still melt in its greasy Day-Glo artificiality over all of the freshness and good things you have gathered, over all of your store, and be the prominent flavor.

Yes, it is possible to cook with it. But if you have good taste (and now you do), throw it out.

The Wonderful

> haul its strange cohesion
> beyond the limits of my vision
> *Christian Wiman*

Sober for almost sixteen days she tells us
the tale of "how much he was trying"— an old ditty
like "he doesn't mean to" and "I just know *if*"—
coffee in hand, staring ahead in long breaths.

Chanel 7 didn't get the bit about trying
between the slow shots: a witness pointing-handtomouth-pointing,
metal shot asunder—the still-glossy pieces growing dim
on the asphalt as the camera shifts away.

Drunks never hit pedophiles or gangbangers;
it's as if Fate carves out the dotted line from loser
to "loving family of four" to place the exclamation
behind *waste* and *pathetic*—

Words she's been swallowing for forty-two years.
Disappointed and disgusted, the nurse says
"Looks like *he* gets to live" pivoting on her white shoes
half-sprint from the blighted kin

"Oh praise Jesus!" she says, "Isn't it wonderful?"
her cold coffee spilling onto glistening linoleum
splashing each of us in its astonishing radius,
stained momentarily in filthy hope.

Son of a Bitch

Five dollars, mama, he'd say and, because it was cheaper
than wondering why, you gave it. Then ten. Then twenty.
I did the best I could, you'd say and, because that seemed
to cover a multitude of sins, he learned the song by heart.
This is for my mama, he'd say, and knock it back in reverence
the first few times. By last call, it came down to, *That bitch.*

This time, you'd say, and he'd promise sobriety and sunshine
and you believed because believing is easier and he would say
I love you, mama, which would get you to pay his rent or lights
and he might even cook you a repast of all of his favorite things
More money, mama, he'd say because most of his favorite things
cost more than you gave and gave less than he wanted, or needed.

This is for my mama, he said when the rest of you died away
and nobody heard or cared and it hit and hurt, *That bitch.*

There Are Times

There are times of tiled floors
and slippers dirtied at the edge
white sunlight against the doors
of cabinets—against the fridge
a cat came and purred and cried
and muzzled the bare white legs
that back-and-forthed as she tried
to fry the rice and fry the eggs—

Powdered hot cocoa, butter
the wet smell of morning—the cold
of 6 a.m., the white fur
of a well-fed feline she'd scold
then slip a burned bacon strip
laughing a little as she
kissed us before our short trip
to school—she'd stand so we could see

Looking back, I'd see her smile
with a fat cat at her feet
and every once in a while
my eyes and hers might meet.

Comadre

You hated each other—that was always clear. You called her whore and, on fitting occasions, your best friend. By turns, she filled a void between husbands. Someone to loathe and crawl into, someone to libel and share your deepest secrets with over lukewarm coffee, stale cookies, and half a dozen offspring making our endless circles around your battlefields and alliances. It was always so exhausting—

She cried for three days when you died. Her son, whom you told me "Watch that one—he will turn on you," circled her in confusion, always looking at me as if to say, "How could she not know? What is the fuss over a woman who would have crushed her if the opportunity ever rose?" We loved each other—the turning son and I. He came to me when she surrendered, told me he was spent, and crawled into bed.

Faraway Words on Jars

Tea leaves, tarot, astrological promises,
      questions about the man you were seeing,
      Filipino? What province? Prick size?
She'd call you *comadre,* give us all

Coffee with Borden's and pandesal
      "Play your games," you said before
      providing Technicolor answers.
She told us take a nap upstairs.

You were gone for three months.
      "This is your father," you called the man
      who wasn't, whose eyes took in
America, LAX, his new wife, us.

There were four more. Always fresh-picked
      from the islands, new last names,
      men like legends
You hoped to label and preserve.

Filipino Food

We leave the head on, bones to pick out;
eating can be a chore, so many utensils
so we go without
                              fingers like kung-fu
(but we're not that kind of Asian) scoop
grey-green mongo beans, bitter melon,

too much garlic, onions in everything, rice
makes one meal last for three. Friends
hate the smell
                              shrimp paste, bright
fuchsia, fishy, they always take too damn
much like that scene in *Joy Luck Club* but

we're not that kind of Asian. We're lesser
so we boast and brag it, every European
spiked our genes
                              but how they recoil,
the descendants come to try out the exotic,
cursed and spit out. They expect Chinese.

Sons of Thunder

Dark enough to wonder
like before faith
or the first time
you try to taste lips

a crowd of boys huddled
for want of warmth
or conspiracy
with cold on words

blown in crystaled breath
against the hard
black wall of night
and blacker shades of trees

and sixth grade boys
crunching hard white
candy ring mints
that clack against teeth

and cut the deep night
and the bits of doubt
that grind in our mouths
to flashes of light.

Passing

I'll answer for it; I kept
        Driving because there is every reason
        To believe the world gave you every opportunity
        To stop, to reassess, to make an awkward u-turn –
        Even if that is not the truth
        A stoplight doesn't afford the space
                To build another person in your place

We didn't end gracefully
        There was much more bleeding
        Much more mess than we – than anyone –
        Could expect (yet we expect
        The mess will clean itself up
        Or dissipate beyond memory)
                So forgive my passing, my averted gaze

You slumped forward, deflated
        Drained in your chair, in that place
        In that husk of a body, hand on the remote
        The television silent as you, as that place –
        And I prayed it wasn't you
        As I walked past the doorframe
                Looking for someone else.

We Were the Tide

or Mom steps onto Long Beach Boulevard

Headlights swerved past you
big and white
small and red
glowing and floating
graceful steel bodies
upstream
downstream
your favorite black negligee
Seagram's 7, your favorite escape
bare feet on asphalt
bare legs in traffic

Twin boys in Underoos, six and skinny
eyes wide open
mouths wide open
waving in the frames between cars
Goodbye
Come back

I have felt the same draw
that solves the jigsaw self
by gathering the pieces
and tossing them away

Come back
Goodbye
We alternate in the aftermath
victim mother
villain mother
Two men in their thirties, stuck on the scene

menaced by your mania
fortified by your fears

constructing our favorite versions
variations on the scope of your destruction

numb to pain
numb to love
graceful steel bodies
glowing and floating
small boy hearts
big boy lives
desperate to swerve past you

Your eyes were looking for him,
your outstretched hands wanting
a man, a life that the tide
ever pulled you from

Goodbye, you said
Come back, we said

Something Significant

Like dying. Easter egg vinegar outside douches
lined up in three colors. Primaries. The Father,
the Son, the Holy Ghost. And tiny plastic robes
to slip around the hard boiled circumference
all condom-like with pictures of Saturday morning
cartoons everyone else has forgotten. Pity.
Especially the shell without fissures. The One
congealed to such inner toughness that holding
the solid weight of it is so assuring. How could we
see how every baptism eats away? That the thin
plastic sheaths—pictures of once-loved heroes
or fantasies unimpressive by today's standard—
were constricting, suffocating. Every beauty
we tried to impart a thorn, a nail, a spear in the side.
In the end, you didn't make the basket showing.
There was only enough, the bright chalky youth
preserved at the center, to whip with pickles,
mayo, smoked paprika. Load into another plastic
bag and squeeze out into Deviled Eggs. Believe me.
The irony of that name. It is not lost. In the end,
you were.

Chow Hall

We drank four glasses of water per meal. Four. Low level impossible.

By comparison, it just really wasn't all that bad and Marines and Army
guys have it so much worse, and they'll tell you so.

Rows of us, bald and scared, hunched over trays, Oliver Twist-like

I joined the Air Force to get away because one more damn day of life
as I was was not an option (but being a cliché was).

Training Instructors, TIs, sat at the front in what was called the Snake Pit

If you did not finish your four glasses of water, some TI would roar,
"Get yer ass on the floor and start pushing, airman!"

We enjoyed the calculated humiliation when it wasn't ours.

Most of us made it through those few weeks. One poor bastard died,
some freak meningitis thing. *Who knew?* No one remembers his name.

Sometimes I drink four glasses of water for my friends.

Each of them could not be more astonished by this ridiculous feat
or the one where I spent four years not being gay. Four.

Aviano, 1996

I see how easy it is to forget –
winter days in Venice: cobblestone streets,
nuns milling beneath a cloister, regret,
cracked stucco walls, large oak doors, our defeat.
What I couldn't tell you then, though I knew
that night you picked me up at the airport,
I could care less for Italy, but you
were the main attraction. Sure, my passport
had a stamp, and the gondolas were cool,
but I only came to discover you.

I'm losing all my memories, you see –
each detail of that trip: your apartment
at the edge of town, Italian coffee –
strong and smooth, hording our every moment...
skiing in Cortina, you patiently
guiding me down the cold and silent path –
stopping in the snow, you looked back at me,
"The answer is: I hope you will not ask."
I never did, and now it is our past.

Windmills

Amstelveen was hotter than
every guide book tableau
and Google image search
had led me to believe

I imagined the opposite for you
who had ambered me, twenty,
full head of hair, in a prime
that withered at the Schipol gates

For three weeks I found a way
to fade into the austere landscape
of little Dutch streets, the Dutch
habit of smiling indifferently,

your tawny boyfriend, twenty,
severe in his opinions, sincere
in recommending the windmills
"All the Americans can't get enough of"

Every penny that flew me to you
told me to tilt toward him,
the youth we spent so cheaply,
but I staid my words

And ran to and from them the next
morning, the late summer sun
already amplifying the age
of my bones, my skin, myself

I had somehow lost halfway
across the Atlantic, hoping for
Amsterdam's famous high
and a reclaimed piece of the past

Below the fan-like blades, sweating
and heaving for air, replaying your
final jab, I had "gotten dumpy," –
a slow and steady, perpetual cutting.

Taking It In

Faded pink buildings squared and desperate
like a line of fingers just losing grip

stranded atop a dark lush lawn the windows
all opaque except the one you flew out

arms elegant, outstretched and your eyes
heavenward as if to draw our own gaze—

blood took its time arriving on scene;
for all we knew you were high again.

"Look," you at Trafalgar Square, staring.

Holbein's canvas was immense, his subject
random, *The Ambassadors*, a globe,

a book of psalms, the anamorphic skull
one must stand at an angle to see.

If We Were Reasonable

Our measure of the monstrous and of the earth-shattering might fall to proportional. Starlight and sun rise should attribute themselves and their services to rotations, latitudes and the invisible line drawn across the equator. Shadows would exist as the afterthought of solid matter rather than reminding us of passing time, lost loved ones, and biblical curses. We could have this conversation again and you would tell me how you didn't mean for it to happen, how this cannot possibly be the end of the world and being overly dramatic is drawing attention to us. You would tell me that you fell in love. Again. And air would still come in through the lungs, the electric flickers of senses would make it to the part of us that reasons and, paradoxically, falls in love. And all of this blood would still be in you. Again.

Rijksmuseum, 2012

Cornered in one frame is a study of falling
Phaethon and Icarus in various angles
making the same plunge

Reached because they wanted sight past
horizon where wiser eyes, wiser hearts
tether us to the seen

Yet an ounce of god-blood or will would rather
crash into the impossible than live
plodding the probable

Cupid, where the winding staircase ends,
holds a finger to his smiling lips
"This will be your master"

He says of the arrows at his fingertips. Feeling
like this is a picture moment, with no one
to take the picture, I know

Something of all the various angles of falling,
why painters, and sculptors, and poets
are always pocketing feathers

The Thing
That Is Dragged

who is the human in this place,
the thing that is dragged or the dragger?

Lucille Clifton, "jasper texas 1998"

The Vertical View of History Holds

Imagine turnip houses, the frail surface bodies
not so much a hint at the sturdy globe below.
All it shows are thin shafts of life, greeny walls
so soft and translucent a warm breath may
pass through like a visiting spirit, airy reminder.

It draws from the fibrous, meaty bulb its spark,
its meaning. It's like the lily shame of Solomon
an earth vine summoning the scythe pulsing
with resplendent stolen source-sap, begging
to be cut down or rooted out, the big reveal.

Leaf house and topsoil sloughed and forgotten,
the world is purple, violet, amethyst, lovely
blue regret gone cold, red memory embrace,
pomme de terre, unearthed fruit, like an apple
offering up the knowledge of remember.

Exit, Cherry Avenue

We were the start of a joke: twin girls, orphans whose furious
hair whipped around the interior of his van, frightened vipers
hungry for a hold; a screaming Mexi-queen, unbuckled, tumbling
in tandem with a Cerberus sized pit bull, the ghettoized version
of Scooby and Shaggy, along for the ride; and up in the front

rigged in place, Rod, our white-faced pilot, paralyzed from two
prior accidents, from the neck down it was mostly will and spasms
propelling all of us from point to point, year to year, navigating
teen confusion, abandonment, the ever-present impotence
echoing through us, "Goddamnit! Goddamnit! My leg is spasming—

"Don't laugh!" Careening down the 405—quadriplegic, dog, girls, me,
the queen—our Mystery Machine gassed by a random muscle, a jerk
like snapping the spine just enough to live, being the only surviving
pup, caught in the stare of unreturned desire, grasping after a mother
grasping her bottle of Schnapps' grasping the irony of it

Oh ye Fates, the sordid act at the dive just off the Cherry Exit, licking
your festering wounds, returning again and again to your all-seeing
eye, the mother tapping the last drop out of that bottle: van, dog, pilot.
Where did you go wrong? Why do your bastard myths always end
with the chilling laughter of those just out of your reach?

Blackface

If the first thing we thought of was Al Jolson singing "Mammy,"
you'd say we were racists, because thinking and doing is the same.
So let me set the stage, out in Long Beach harbor, a rental boat
stuffed with thirty-too-many of our clan, the crackerest crackers,
sweating in mid-October because of course it's hot, and, well,

we're fat, and we can say that because we are (and you try passing
up Costco's three-dollar pizza, churro, and large soda combo—
didn't think so). No one knew she was dead for a week. Neighbors
were all Chinks and Mexicans. I can't say Chinks? Who the hell
is telling this goddamn story anyhow? We were sweatin', wailing

like Jesus himself died again. Sure, we had drank some, beer or two
but it was mostly the missing her, the guilt of missing her death,
seeing her poor boy, Billy. We knew the story. Not right to tell it
here. But his dad was his uncle if you catch my meaning. There he was.
looking all sad and angry. His cousins, the twins, too...

*Why the hell did we come to this, Shon? We didn't even like that piece
of shit! They burned her with her cats. All of the them. There are two
whole bags of ashes. I don't know. They said we were going to drop
the ashes in the harbor but we are pretty far out. Why are we so far?
Just let me yell up and see where we are going.*

It's nothing like the movies. No sheet of ashes spreading out like birds
the way they do when the sun is setting. Just two clumps of dark dust,
one bolting to the water, the other landing right on Shannan, Joy's
uppity twin daughter. Damned if she didn't look just like Al Jolson!
I said, "Say Mammy!" Those girls never come 'round. Forget family.

I Would

I would die for touch, for an embrace
to lull me through the dark of it
and recall in the feeding hour
of the worm and mushroom taking
root in my sacrifice.

I would give my final breath for a delicate
hope suspended, floating inside
of the last escape pod to be shot
across the black universes
to land on the distant bright sands
of a distant dark time
when a reflection of me stumbles
and gasps, thirsty for it.

I would, willingly, go to the knife—
"A far better thing..." I would say
winking at God who would now
be in my debt, and I would smile
to the adoring crowd who rushed
me to destruction, worshipping
what they made, loved, and killed
as we so often do, the masochists
and arsonists that we are: watching
in glee the sacrifice wrapped
in the liquid flames, the jelly blood
glistening, the sweet smell
of flesh on a spit...

I would die, I guess,
for whatever feeds
on my pieces.

Deluge

white-trash girl walking ten steps in front of me
coconut lotion and pink skin in her wake
hallway crumbling into Atlantic Avenue
Church's Chicken, the porn shop in purple
paint with a movie marquee like the one
in front of Jordan High School—Congratulations
Graduating Class of 1993—and Sal's
the old Mexican barber who still used pomade,
made small talk about Clinton, the weather,
hottest summer in Carmelitos, every fat
mother porched and screaming, "Kesha! Dexter!
Tee!" who never answered but stood or danced
in line for snow cones at the Mae twins
front door, a nickel and pretending to
know who was Mae Belle and Mae Mae,
neither made it to Jordan in 89 when Cody's
mom sent him to doom in a Billabong shirt,
fresh-permed hair and an uncomfortably long
kiss goodbye out there on Atlantic, her
pink fingernails, the faux-leopard jacket, blue
Camaro, cigarettes and coconut lotion,
"Bye bye, baby! Do good!"
mortified, his pout-lips and red-cheeks,
that perm! eyes scanning for some crevice
to crawl between and wait out four years...

In the Ball Crawl

The best years of my life I spent a rat
Hired for three summers to be Chuck E. Cheese
After the second time I applied
After my friend, Cody, put in a good word –
Cody is white.
I slipped into a matted gray body suit.

The best years of my life I spent a rat
Happy to token my group, happy to Franklin
Our Peanuts gang on campus
And in all the pictures
I was never white.
The suit always smelled like the last Chuck E.

The best years of my life I spent a rat
Cody was my best friend and I hated him
So much that I wanted nothing more
Than to be him.
Outside fluff, inside the ripe sweat of hours.

The best years of my life I spent a rat
Ratting along the intricate
Labyrinthine tunnelry of angst
And rat rage.
I wore a hollow head.

The best years of my life I spent a rat
Watching him through eyes
Of rude-cut metal mesh
Scraping my inner face raw.
Giant rat hands that felt nothing...

The best years of my life I spent a rat
Capable of scrounging up
A meal, but happy to leftover,
Crumb, swallow up –
Shuck and jive in the ball crawl.

How to Be (I)

The white male poet I hate and want to be
writes everything in series with the same titles
because coming up with more words is so passé.

I probably should mention he's a bit of a hipster—
goes without saying he's so damn handsome is the problem.
Hell, I read his stuff just to pretend

I could have coffee with him. See him in the flesh,
imbibe the one thing of value. The white. The beauty. The white
hot him so hard to cleave from his poems.

I picture his hands writing them, his soft pink mouth
speaking them, his green-blue eyes scanning the lines. From some
objective point of view, he writes all about brown skin and black skin

and broken people and broken hearts. And hearts are not colored.
Hearts are all the same. That's what he says. That's what his poems say,
picture his beautiful white face, pink lips, his words as my own.

How to Be (II)

He calls me at 3 AM and tells me about his latest
inspiration and the poem she has birthed. "We,"
he says, "have to collect our poems everywhere."
He tells me this as if I were his child, his mentee,
his sous-chef and shadow, though I out rank him
in age and experience and, to be honest, hunger.

"Let me read you what I have" and he does so
and for two and a half hours—I never hang up
because he has seeded himself all over the damn place
and I am looking for his secret—he does so.
I always feel cheap when he gets off. But that's it,
he just gets off. One of us satiated. Whore.

This is how the poem goes. It always goes this way:
"I met a woman who possessed everything I felt
lacking inside of me. I invited her back to mine, let
her feel safe with me long enough to extract what I
needed. I know it's wrong, but writing it here
absolves me of all wrong. She never had it so good."

How to Be (III)

He hated that post I made about Ferguson. "You can't honestly,"
he says, "buy into that crap? That the white man is to blame
for all evil in this world? I mean, you know me and I'm not
a racist. I just think" and he goes on to tell me what he thinks.

We have known one another longer than I can remember. Once,
I thought of us as cut from the same poverty-smeared cloth. He
wore hand-me-downs, some worse than mine. Twice a week he
ate at my house to dodge an abusive step-father and his mother

who treated him like Christ. Every day, right in front of school,
she'd hold his face in her hands and say, "You're the best thing
I ever did in this world." She'd kiss him on both of those boyish
cheeks, flush in embarrassment and her coral-red lipstick. He ran

as quick as he could from her to find me. "I can't get her to stop
doing that. I hate it so much" and he'd go on to tell me how much.
My mother was the same. She would have done it, too, but we
didn't have a car. But I wasn't talking about my mother. I was

talking about his mother. His life. It always seemed to matter
so much more. "One of these days," he would say to me, "you
are going to write the story of our life. About my crazy mom,
me and you. I believe in you." Which is why I started writing.

How to Be (IV)

I dated white John. I think I knew
it wouldn't work.
We were doing that thing that new couples do
where they ask one another
seemingly pointless questions

"What is your biggest fear?"
"What is your grandest dream?"

Not innocuous volleys, the arc of intention
targeted me, Magic 8-Ball
me to shake vigorously, anticipating the perfect words.
"I want a house," I said
and he laughed.

"A house is not a real dream," as fact
"Everyone will eventually have a house."

After that, I couldn't stop hearing him laugh. White woman
hands me her bags at the airport,
white man ask if I speak English (I teach it), I catch
all the piercing laughter.

Dumbo the Flying Elephant

The first flight was awkward and exhilarating –
Watching my shadow fused to yours, two bodies lifted
High above the prismatic fantasyland of possibilities,
Unaware of my ability to make you rise or fall
We enjoyed each other passively
For a short moment we travelled
Went nowhere
Landed

And the day wore on so quickly, the attractions outpacing
One another in mystery, in glamour, in agility, experience –
And my appetite and imagination rose
To the pirates and the cowboys,
The haunted corners
The doomed artifacts
Left me
Breathless

How far have I been since I stretched out my arms
And you stretched out your ears, and we
Flew above it all – the strange mountain range
Below us filled with danger and dark places,
Wild animals, wild gods, outer space
Swirling just beneath the surface
Calling me
Away

But I watched you from afar, just out of sight, out of reach
Today – and a few times before, to tell the truth –
Giving yourself over to the will of other novices
Fumbling at the joystick, ignorant of the ways
To make you rise and fall –
I see the magic of it
Wonder why
We end

Contiguous We

Aisle 5, coffee and cereal, she reading
green label guarantee the Ugandan they
pick holly-like beads clustered, close—
they are safe, she is safe, coffee is
free trade, free thought, on sale.

She says *Please* to me, to help, to say
Which would to answer *Whichever*
pick with your heart or, make it easy
go with the gut, get both, move on
Mexico in produce, Chile in canned

We she says thumbing Southern Living—
"German Christmas Cookies, Grandma
Good!"—*always seem to forget one
thing or the other!* cashier he greets we
without a glance up, hands moving

Coffee in grip, pause, loudspeaker, *We
still have this special* faceless she *yes*
both half price, that's one free he figures,
he says so, he smiles, she misses—
his hand on the bag, on mine, we.

Wonderland

Club 1350, Long Beach, California

Tonight I want to go to hell, I want
to know there are Hearts more rock
than the granite in me. Down
Anaheim Street, the yellow dandelion street lights
spread more sparingly in the rear view,
the city reaches—like a garden
of hungry blossoms and weeds—to me.

I'm going to hell, past Wilmington
where all is mechanical and rust
to Club 1350, a black wall, a rabbit hole
grafted to night, to sea water stench, to dark.
I'm going to hell, like Alice, who talks
To doors that warn:
"This is a Private Club, you may be asked
to leave" and I think how odd,

After all this time, hell still tries to imitate
heaven. Poor Hearts. I pray for them
shoving behind me, rushing to doom,
to some other wonder land—
The upper level of hell has lockers
to keep families and clothes locked up, mirrors
dripping streams of steam and no one looks through them.
Naked men, winter pale like rabbits or white roses.

They have no eyes—eyes are for love, eyes are
for heaven—just penises, pendulums
reminding you that *you're late!* No matter,
Hell is eternal.
Stairs sink to the next level, lit
on the sides like movie theater isles

and naked wanting bodies usher me
to the Queen's Court...

It is hell's second level and stinks of bleach and cum
of sweat and shit, decapitated Hearts and hunger, foul
from being so long in this dark, here
where it fermented and crawls up black walls,
On tiles where bare feet and asses lift it
on to the white bleached sheets, under
the angels, the Hearts, the ones
I need to see...

Body over body, indistinguishable,
some nightmare Nazi-camp deck of bodies, stacked
still groans, still sweats and shivers, cold
in the black walls pierced with glory holes;
The red diamond lights and the porn showing
the Hearts how the angels do it, and they
do it, staring through the looking glass,
at me, and I know they don't see...

On the Dance Floor

If the world hates you...

I
This is the wide way
This is the wayward way
The dance floor
Polished in spilt martinis, a glass
Reflecting the light and the beat
And the bodies on the floor
On verge to burst with release
        Of hours spent with secrets
Kept silent like serpents
That sweep the sand

        Road without end, path to nowhere
        expanse, the eternal treadmill

        Dancers who met here
To hook up and fuck in night's many corners
Remember the floor—the beat—the way
That begins in Sodom and Corinth
And is the wide way
The wayward way.

II
Dancers that dream and dare
Not open their eyes in the Corners
Where joy ends in an ahhhh...
Corners where dancers die
Like the God of Gods died
With the blade of a kiss
And hang only
Limp hands without protest, that wish
The dream that lied...
"If only, if only..."

Lead me not into
The Corners, night's cold corners
Let me wear drag
Become the dream queen
Red pucker lips, false hips, fake hair, tits
The Madonna
Blessing the unrepentant
In corners—

                Not the final act
        in the Wayward Way Bar.

III
This is the dream land
This is Fantasyland
Here the smoke and strobe
Lights lift go-go angels
On cold, steel poles to be worshiped
By the dancers in the holy light of Ecstasy
                called *piece of heaven*
Sold by the tab in corners
Of empty space
Or last-night's-muscle-boy-beat-me-fantasy—
Stoned like Stephen
Dying in our own church without mourners—
A swallow to keep the pace.

IV
The dancers are not here
Nobody dances here
On the shore of the dried-up dream
On this bankrupt bank
This used, torn condom in the corner

        In this last dance on the floor
We reach together to each other
Voiceless, mouthing prayers

By Cher, our holy, Holy Mother

     Abandoned, except
The dancers return
As the Fantasy
The vine
Like arms to wrap around
The Corner's shadows
and love them.

V
Someday I'll wish upon a star
And wake up where the clouds are far
Behind me

     After the song
And the sex
After the sweat
And the regret
Comes the prayer

                    Have mercy on me, O God

     After the fix
And the fall
After the addiction
And the program
Comes the prayer

                        Night is very dark

     After the idol
And the sin
After the hunger
And the taste
After the plunder
And the prison
Comes the prayer

                    Have mercy on me, O God

Have mercy on
Night is
Have mercy on me

This is the way the evening ends
This is the way the evening ends
This is the way, this is the wide way.

"You Gonna Be Up All Night"

the black preacher on midnight radio warns
an emmm-hmming congregation
who might challenge him about, "Don't nowhere
in the Bible say ten percent..." and he
laughing at their ignorance
says again, "You gonna be up all night!"
as I've decided against the porn and the dark room
of empty motions
and turned him on for a reprieve,
some easy grace about superhero Jesus
swooping down to hand me my mat and say, "Walk!"
this is not what I wanted

to hear him tell it, I think to myself, now searching
through a million body frieze pages, to hear
him laughing all oooh-hoo "I'm tell-ing, you... yeees, sir!"
God's got a sense of humor at least

live-chat rooms have that nostalgic 90s thing
when I'd type myself into an adult, experienced
enough to catch the innuendo, "I'd like to log onto *you*!"
so I pause when the offer blinks over the Coach
who just told a shirtless teammate, "How can I
keep you on the team, son?"
and he's shirtless, too, because he knows
there's gonna be hell to pay. But the memory
passes and I click to close the screen
but it misses and turns him back on
out of sight, just his voice under the teammate, under the Coach
"You gonna be up all night! Yeees, sir!"

One Whole Voice That Is You

read about *yawp* and promised to do so
to gather pounds of air, build the pressure
pumping now and then bellows
that fan out small prayer

       to the wingspan of foolish, foolish
hope that is ever launching from you in dreams.
You wake up reaching out and calling to it,
your fledgling words tripping and falling.

Gather them unto you once more and love
their frailty to *forte*, build up confidence
with slightly altered lore of sound and song
that shaped the world

       and all that is in it, the graceful silences
that glide along the deep, crawling murmurs
craning their prehistoric necks to glimpse
full-throated *Yes* gliding overhead.

Hundreds of Smaller Deaths

I want to know whose idea this was,
filling up death
with hundreds of smaller deaths.

Charles Jensen, "Flowers"

Mamertinum: Sheol[1]

How far away the day seems and his voice
    "I see heaven"[2] and casting a cloak at my feet,
    they build the silence
    upon him – this rock –
    I know you by your garment,
    I cannot say if you are butler or baker
But remember me, here, remember!
    Let me die
    I shall forget the drop of anguish
    That scalds me now
    That scalds me now![3]
What whiteness will you add?
    She is washing her hands in dreams again[4]
    Stare, stare in the basin
    Like Pilate before the crowd[5],
    and wonder what you missed[6]
    What would you have me do?
    What whiteness will you add?
Back to Damascus,
'tis good you know not that you are his heirs,
for if you should, O, what would come of it?[7]
    Saul, Saul
Última de morir crucificado,
oyó, entre los escarnios de la gente,
que el que estaba muriéndose a su lado
era Dios.[8]
    Don't bullshit me – a man on whom the sun has gone down –
    Saul, Saul
    Why are you persecuting me?
Back to Damascus –
O Ananias, let me see more than Rome, more than Taishan spread out
I dream myself on a silver platter[9]
O Ananias, let me see
    "I see heaven"
Don't bullshit me – I see my tragedy written in thy brows[10]

(A man may see how this world goes with no eyes)[11]
Mais, il devint orgueilleux et plein d'arrogance; alors il fut renversé
de son trône royal et privé de sa gloire.[12]

> What is it worth? What is it worth to know so much of this world
> that old oceans and lovers rock me out of peace,
> thorn me into conscious dying?
> O Timothy, the young man
> reveres men of genius, because
> to speak truly, they are more
> himself than he is.[13]
> I know you by your garment,

My time is coming soon
sing songs of transformation:

> You are ever seeing, never perceiving –
>> Want to swallow up gilded fruit
>>> You are ever listening, never hearing
>>>> Through your beastly ears[14]
>>>>> Wherein the scenes of Greece and Rome
>>>>> Had all the commonplace of home[15]

Closing my eyes to resurrect
light that set my course
in blindness –
This floor becomes the metaphor – Upon this rock
where men etched a final wish
some view our sable race with scornful eye/ "Their colour
is a diabolic die."
Don't bullshit me –
Remember, Christians, Negroes, black as Cain/ May be refin'd, and join
th' angelic train[16]

> Heroism is exhausting, yet
> it contradicts a greed[17]

In misfortune, even death,
encourages others
and in its defeat, stirs
the soul to be strong![18]

> I don't know how humanity stands it
> Oh, hold me up a little! I shall go away i'the jest else.[19]

I consider my life worth nothing to me

if only I may finish the race
if only I may finish[20]
(Let me die, let me die, let me die, let me die, let me die)
O Timothy, if you could hear the birds, like jingle bells
like jingle bells and jazz:

> *Comme te po' capì chi te vò bene*
> *si tu le parle 'mmiezzo americano?*
> *Quando se fa l 'ammore sotto 'a luna*
> *come te vene 'capa e di:"i love you!?"*[21]

It does return
language to bring us back, to bring back
Who thou lovest broken
Who thou lovest blindly
Who thou lovest best
It does return with the birds, with language, with...

> "I see heaven!"
> Then waltzed me off to bed
> Still clinging to your shirt[22]

It does return...
"You therefore, my son, be strong..."[23]

Mamertinum: Barnabas[24]

Questi comandamenti, che oggi ti do, ti staranno
nel cuore; li incilchera ai tuoi figli,
ne parlerai quando te ne starai seduto in casa tua,
quando sara per via
quando ti coricherai
quando ti alzerai[25]
      – not of one bird but of many

Ich glaubte als kind   *When I consider Your heavens[26]*
dass die menschen brüder sind
auch wenn sie so oft
einander nicht verstehn
heut weiss ich: der hass
macht die menschen bös und blind
und doch glaub ich fest daran
es kann so nicht weiter gehn[27]
      At Ἀντιόχεια ἡ ἐπὶ Δάφνη[28], perhaps I lost myself
      So eager I was to tell them of the Good News
      I lost myself and you, my true friend[29], I lost
Einmal   *The work of Your fingers*
nach tausend kriegen
nach blut und tränen
lernen wir doch
dann wird
man leben statt hassen
und leben lassen[30]
      Enkidu Patroclus Jonathan Barnabas Kerouac
      what did I know, What did I know,
      of love's austere and lonely offices[31]
Einmal   *The moon and stars*
nach tausend schlachten
wird man sich achten
selbst in gefahr
menschen
müssen doch menschlich sein

unfehlbar
wird es einman wahr[32]

    Ye may not know how desolate
    are bosoms rudely forced to part[33]
    caressing the filthy floor like a cheekbone, like a lip
    Saul, Saul
    why are you persecuting me?
    Perhaps I lost myself...
    I lost...

Einmal   *Which You have ordained*
nach tausend kriegen
nach blut und tränen
lernen wir doch
dann wird
man leben statt hassen
und leben lassen

    The development of the angels:
    mutilated people will float around like mutilated leaves[34]
    don't you see that we are better for being broken?

niemand kann   *What is man –*
die hoffnung töten
macht uns die angst auch stumm und bleich[35]

    From plots and treasons Heaven preserve my years,
    but save me most from my petitioners.
    Unsatiate as the barren womb or grave;
    God cannot grant so much as they can crave[36] –
    Perhaps I lost myself

Von dem Gott, zu dem wir beten[37]

    It was you that broke the new wood[38]

sind wir menschen alle gleich[39]

    We were together since the War began.   *Alle gleich.*
    He was my servant – and the better man[40].   *Alle gleich.*

Wir alle...
Einmal   *That You take thought of him?*
nach hoffen und fragen
nach mut und versagen
wird irgendwann klar
mensch sein

heisst anderen nah zu sein
heisst verzeihn
dann wird unfehlbar
was auch war...[41]

If I speak with the tongues of men and of angels,
but do not have love[42]

> Birds sing to me at night – the rain, the sun, the changing
> seasons are new friends
> Solitude is a hard won ally, faithful and patient[43]

Der traum...

> If I have the gift of prophecy and know all mysteries
> and all knowledge
> But do not have love

Einmal...

> If I give my possessions to feed the poor, if I surrender
> my body to be burned
> But do not have love

Der traum...einmal...

> It profits me nothing

Der traum...einmal...wahr

> What did I know? What did I know?

Mamertinum: Silas

Make-strong old dreams lest this our world lose heart[44]
They tell me in dream languages
    this one short day be forgetful of your children
    afterwards weep; for even though you will kill them,
    they were very dear –[45]
keep at the wall, in the dark, keep at the wall
record of the days
    no skill in the world
    nothing human can penetrate the future[46]
lovely they are, alight on the barbed wire
Muses over the mesh and airstrip
    I went from door to door
    I was wild with God – I heard them call me
    "Beggar! Wretch! Starve for bread in hell!"[47]
Listen to me! Pardon me
I lost myself
    "Sweet Spirit, what souls are these?"[48]
Humans are (can be) conduits of extraordinary things,[49]
record of the days
Do you have the madeleines? I keep on forgetting[50]
    you will not find it there but in/ despised poems.
    it is difficult/ to get the news from poems
    yet men die miserably every day/for lack
of what is found there.[51]
Where, past the inverted glass pyramid and Winged Victory[52]
serving as a sign post, and just beneath
what is left of Dieudonné[53]
for while I was passing through and examining the objects of your
    worship,
I also found an altar with this inscription,
    Νή τόν Ἄγνωστον[54]
What therefore you worship in ignorance
je viens vous l'annoncer[55]
        What is man?
Lovely they are

the bells from île de la Cité
Sonnez les matines! Sonnez les matines!
lives of great men all remind us
we can make our lives sublime
Sonnez les matines! Sonnez les matines!
and, departing, leave behind us
footprints on the sands of time.[56]
They tell me in dream languages
write if you must
only if you must
you must[57]

      "You've been at it all night."
      "Don't bullshit me"
      "O Timothy!"
          "O Barnabas!"
      "O Silas!"
Let me die, let me die, let me die, let me die
"Aren't you a Pharisee?"
"No, he's a Sadducee!"
      "O Timothy!
          "O Barnabas!"
      "O Silas!"
Keep your eye on those
who cause dissensions and hindrances
contrary
to the teaching which you learned
turn away from them.[58]
      "No, he's a poet!"
      "Ha!"
(Ah why did I mix
my best sayings with their
idle chatter? While outside
unschooled people were walking around
thirsty for instruction)[59]
Hugo called them butterflies – the scraps of unfinished works,
      love letters
I tore when my hunger would have more than I could crave
      "Poet!"

but the fiber of those sheets – how could you know? –
would save whole generations

the best of artists can no concept find
that is not in a single block of stone

Keep at the wall, in the dark

confined by the excess; to that alone
attains the hand obedient to the mind[60]

Keep at the wall, in the dark

Somebody embroidered the doily
Somebody waters the plant,
Or oils it, maybe. Somebody
Arranges the rows of cans
So that they softly say:
ESSO-SO-SO-SO
To high-strung automobiles.[61]

The work of Your fingers
tell them the languages of dreams.

Mamertinum: Rhizome[62]

太 初 有 道 、 道 與 　 神 同 在 、 道 就 是 　 神[63]
only time to think here
time to think, try not to forget –
one does not explain away what is already done
one does not argue against what is already accomplished
one does not condemn what has already gone by[64]
    That is to say...
the poet's function is not to report things that have happened
but rather to tell of such things as might happen
things that are possibilities   *The moon and the stars...*
by virtue of being, in themselves,

                    Which You have ordained
Inevitable... Probable... [65]
    literature is not inimical to ideas – it thrives upon them! But...[66]
have we gone to the books already? Don't you see
the metaphor rising in the east? Can we not
start with that?
    Onomatopoeia might be used to prove
    that the choice of the signifier is not always
arbitrary?[67]
    Marx Freud Gramsci Benjamin Lacan Lévi-Strauss
    built the structures teaming with corners
    and minotaurs
Where is the string?
Where are my feathers?
Wouldn't it be better to schizophrenize?[68]
    The greatest value would be at the same time the least
    kept in reserve. Nature's resources would be expended
    without depletion, exchanged without labor
                   Der traum...
Freely given, exempt from
                  Einmal...
Masculine transactions: enjoyment without a fee
               Der traum...einmal...
Well-being without pain, pleasure without possession[69]

And Caliban?

There is no way of putting this euphemistically –

irrational, depraved (fallen), childlike, "different" – *a Pharisee!*

And Darcy?

Rational, virtuous, mature, normal – also, a Pharisee.[70]

Sinners

(among whom I am foremost of all).[71]

Do you have the madeleines?

Mamertinum: Timothy

Thar was the batell dangerus and strong;
Gret was the pres, bath perellus and throng.[72]

Picture them at that long last supper
sporting their da Vinci robes
arms outstretched but do not touch
the hand or heart of one another
as the conversation flows,
"He tried too little, and he too much."

How should we term your dealings to be just,
If you unjustly deal with those that in your justice trust?[73]

These, the kings and mighty leaders,
these the clutch of fallen crowns
await arrival of another:

Who shall absolve the foulness of their fate, -
Those doomed, conscripted, unvictorious ones?[74]

He held his lover in the waters
drowning out the sound of hounds,
of horses, of the blind brother
gripping tight a hunting spear –   *What is man?*
"There," Ailill cries, brokenhearted,
"A specimen of noble breed,
and the shot to him is clear!"[75]

Here is the adrenaline rush you crave,
That inexorable flight, that insane puncture...[76]

a king goes down, his soul departed –

Arbitrary?

a soul arrives with timeless speed.

Yet time serves wherein you may redeem
Your banished honors and restore yourselves
Into the good thoughts of the world again[77]

"Welcome, Fergus, to the never-ending
feast of fallen, foolish men,"
says Arthur, handing him a grail,   *That You take thought of him?*
"Yes, that's Achilles – his wound is mending,
try to avoid *wise* Solomon...
so, how, exactly did *you* fail?"

What are you doing down there,
Among woebegone humanity, the plaything of fate?[78]
"There are no righteous wars"[79]
I heard from a pacifist wielding the picture of some destruction
he blamed on me – and why not? What did I know
of the Crusades and the Slaves and the Religious Right?
How could I know I would penetrate the future?

Mamertinum: Aftermath[80]

What hubris, I think, to say to oneself
"How dare he label me what I am!"
      "Timothy!
"Barnabas!"
        "Boise!"[81]
It is an abomination
caressing the filthy floor like a cheekbone, like a lip
      "I knew you read the *Symposium* during the vac,
      then you understand
      without me saying more?"
"How do you mean?"
      "I love you."
"Oh rot!
Durham, you're an Englishman. I'm another. Don't talk nonsense.
I'm not offended, because I know you don't mean it...

                  If I have not love

But it's the only subject absolutely beyond the limit
as you know,
it's the worst crime in the calendar
you must never mention it again"[82]

                O Ananias, let me see more

      Beautiful, tragical faces,

              When I consider Your heavens

Ye that were whole, and are so sunken;
and, O ye vile, ye that might have been loved
that are so sodden and drunken,
      who hath forgotten you?[83]
      To balance me out so I live in what's left of
      the evidence not out there in the rotting
      garden the firebombed street and Plato's myth
      of lovers the fated meeting of equal halves[84]
        O wistful, fragile faces, few out of many!
      "Timothy!
"Maurice!"
      "Boise!"

The gross, the coarse, the brazen,
God knows I cannot pity them, perhaps, as I should do,
but, oh, ye delicate, wistful faces,
     who hath forgotten you?
     "Did you really not know even for a minute?"
"How could I know? You seem just like...you know, normal
how could I know?![85]
     He would not stay for me; and who can wonder?
     He would not stay for me to stand and gaze.
     I shook his hand, and tore my heart in sunder,
     And went with half my life about my ways.[86]
If I have not love
what shadows we can cast with the best of intentions
how far away the day seems and his voice
     and the beer is kneading us into strange embraces,
     like Greek wrestlers whose arms, in those paintings
     they show us in school, in the Stars' frozen poses,
     are arms that could be strangling the opponent,
     could be holding tight the lover![87]
     "Jackson!"
"Maurice!"
     "Boise!"
That from the gates of death,
     that from the gates of death: Whitman[88] calls me back
not till the sun excludes you do I exclude you,
not till the waters refuse to glisten for you and the leaves to rustle
for you,
do my words refuse to glisten and rustle for you.[89]
And words are all that is left
and the filthy floor I've kissed, caressed, love
scratched out my proclamation "To pull the thorn – that is a start!"[90]
     (What hubris, I think)
Who thou lovest in innuendo
Who thou lovest in dangerous glances
               It does return
                      What is man –

As the story goes,
     Jonathan made a covenant with David

because he loved him –
Jonathan stripped his robe, his armor,
his sword, his bow, his belt
and gave it to David[91]
because he loved him –
"Whatever you say, I will do."[92]
My time is coming soon
Whatever is true, whatever is honorable,
whatever is right, whatever is pure,
whatever is lovely, whatever is of good repute, if there is any excellence
if anything is worthy of praise
dwell on these[93]

What are you doing down there,
Among woebegone humanity, the plaything of fate?
Let me die, let me die, let me die – oh let an old man rest[94]
O Barnabas
O Timothy
O Silas

Je viens vous l'annoncer   *That You take thought of him?*
In the quiet final hours, no birds or gods or cannon
just a pang deep in the pit of me for a morsel of you
a small, good thing[95]
to see me through
the dark of it.[96]

Stars

...it grows such sweet things out of such corruptions.

Matt, Wyoming, 1998:
Night in Laramie,
the play ended an hour ago, the light from town is low,
my wearied friends sleep, wrapt in the last moment of it—
a modern day ex machina,
Angel, beautiful, suspended from translucent spider threads,
Angel proclaiming God's love to the broken, diseased, dying—
it was
a happy ending...

I look at the stars, which I have never noticed 'til tonight:
pageantry of mythical men forever chasing, forever hunting,
forever seeking to slay their individual beasts who, with them, with me,
populate Wyoming pitch and winter's black, frozen pond—
they remind us that the struggle goes on and is timeless,
the battle never ending.

Do you look back at me, Stars? Do you dance to seduce me to you?
Gussied with silver? I see how your passion for me burns across galaxies
and I am reaching back and I am burning, burning at the edge
of Wyoming in October
as the snow reflects the beauty of my blaze
and tonight I will reach back to you, I will
find one of you
here on earth...

darest thou now O soul,
walk out with me toward the unknown region,
where neither ground is for the feet nor any path to follow?[97]

What leads my feet to town, to Laramie, tonight?
What desire born within, rising by command
of the Moon's bone-white turning eye,

his captivating magic eye mesmerizing the great waters' ebb and flow,
mesmerizing my own ebb and flow?
and these Stars!

These handsome legend warriors,
these cowboys of the galaxies,
my evening comrades and friends,
where do you lead me? Down what unlit path do I follow your calling?

Wyoming is alive tonight! And Matt is alive tonight!
The electricity of the neon sign above the snow,
Fireside Lounge[98] it flashes and beckons in bubble gum pink
and you Stars, you encouragers toward corruption
and band of plotting cohorts that gather in the corners of winter night!
You will be my destruction, friends!
You who my father and I would watch[99] and he would tell me

"These are the true friends, Matt,
these are the friends who won't betray you"
And we were companions, you Stars and I—
No. We are more, my Stars
We are lovers, we are light hungry for light, hungry for reunion.
We share the black field of the prairie sky,
we hunt the beasts ever out of reach,
it is all we know to trust the light, responding light, of one another,

and I did trust you, even tonight
I trusted your prodding here.

There is no unreturn'd love, the pay is certain one way or another[100]

I sing the song of Aaron[101]!
Let me sing of my love unrequited!
Let me sing of him, my Error!
This is cowboy country, it is in the cornbread tan of your neck
where the stark white t-shirt ends and you begin,
a beautiful you begins! and you're laughing at my drunkunfunny jokes,
your warm breath close to my face, the smell of cigarettes and beer,

74

and the beer is kneading us into strange embraces, like Greek wrestlers
whose arms, in those paintings they show us in school, in the Stars'
frozen poses,
are arms that could be strangling the opponent,
could be holding tight the lover!

We never really know,
do we? Those faces from the paintings never tell us
what one man is saying to the other man in those first moments
or those last moments...*you want to leave? But where? And why?*

Night in Laramie,
the drive ended hours ago, the light from the town is low,
you were the beast never meant to be snared,
you were the god too high to touch no matter the height
of the tower or need,
and destruction is eminent, I know, when we reach for the divine,
but we reach, against Nature, or, perhaps *by* Nature, we reach...

I sing the song of Aaron!
Why? My would-be-lover, my cowboy, my Aaron!
The stars led me to you! The stars brought you out, too!
They and you, my friends and my lost love—Betrayers!
Shall I list my pains as the taillights fade away?
Not the thunder clap thud of the pistol,
not the taste of your skin crumbs left in my mouth
not the fists like typewriter arms
rising and falling, imprinting the story of our night together,
not the *faggot, faggot, faggot* song you hissed in my ear
like a lover as you tied my hands and feet,
not the prod of the deer fence against my naked back,
not the cold, not the cold that is slowing
the world to a beat, beat
...beat

But our last embrace, Aaron!
No one will know, no one will believe!

The things that we say! The things that men say
in those last cruel moments!

Walt Whitman in Wyoming, 1998:
I think this face is the face of the Christ himself[102]

Look down fair Moon [103]and shame your Stars!
See how they have brought another out into the winter night!
See how they envied their fallen comrade! And made to put him out!
One touch of your bloodied hand to mine O boy...
can you, in this last sleep, hear Walt Whitman?
The prairie night and my voice will sing you to eternity:

See how they sleep?[104] See how your mother's whisper of love
is for *you*, boy?
How it settles in the down pillow, and the dreams and the prayers
settle, too?
And they rest for tomorrow, when you will alter their course
and purpose,
and the death of you, for you will die, will launch a thousand
whispers from the mouths and pillows
of all the other sleepers who feared
to let them go...
You are the catalyst,
You are the Christ whose death will bring life—

Matt is alive tonight! Matt is alive in the bare branches whose veins
are burning with the thought of spring! Matt is alive in the prairie
grasses crawling toward a sun they only see in dreams!

Matt is alive in the wary deer who wanders
To his hand, licks it, and knows the better fate of those leaping spirits
caught in such traps!
Matt is alive in the brimming dawn!

Matt is alive in the frenzied pace of the Laramie police station where a
call comes in from a biker by the roadside! *Yes, biker, I, too saw beauty
crushed at the first light of day!*

Matt is alive in the friends waking to his horrible absence!

Matt is alive in the phone hanging from a cord and a mother collapsed
on the cool tiles of her kitchen floor! *Forgive me! I held him though I
knew it was your place in the pieta, mother!*

Matt is alive in a song, a song that plays over and over, over and over
as a once-handsome-cowboy walks the long, never-ending halls
and remembers those final words! *Aaron! Aaron! What idol can you
erect[105] in your solitude? Will it resemble the Moon? The Stars? Him,
telling you his final song?*
Will it pardon you to live longer than those words?
Matt is alive in a prairie thunder that echoes in New York and San
Francisco[106] and 'round the wide, wide world!

And that will be your history, son of responding kisses
Your bruised face and slight body, and golden hair
Catching the sun will give you the likeness of a star
And that is what you will be,
A messenger to the wide world of upward lookers:
Those who wonder at the names and allegiances of stars.

Me in Texas, tonight:
*You came, taciturn, with nothing to give—but we looked on each other,
When lo! more than all the gifts of the world you gave me[107].*
And look! Even now, these words of mine,
And the words of whole generations
Amorous after you, our would-be-lover,
Our brother, our comrade and muse—

*The powerful play goes on, and you,
Sweet you, contribute this verse!*[108]

We are alive tonight! The Stars, The Everlasting shine—
"These are the true friends, Matt
The friends who won't betray you"—
That you exist, and eternity...

The Look
into the Canyon

The trouble was not about finding acceptance.
Acceptance was available in the depths of the mind
And among like people. The trouble was the look into the canyon
Which had come a long time earlier
And spent many years being forgotten.

Adrienne Su, "Adolescence"

The Far Reaches of What Humans Can Find

for Sissy

white gloss hallways remind me of *Star Wars*
when badass Vader emerges from dry ice
black cape flowing, heavenly and grim
all the dark side of diagnosis

you scratching out the route to the escape pod
maybe knowing me in the way Leia told Luke
"I think I always did" in the *final episode*
never saw the prequel coming

you of your youth preserved by friends
bound up in *Stupid Hope*, a new hope
balancing in my nervous grip there
with the bright walls sans droids or lasers

just the confusions multiplying
on the other side of doors where big words
make as much sense as Jar Jar Binks
but we cannot wish away what is

finally, she emerges like Han from the carbonite
losing only a small piece of breast, some hair
but what is that when a wrinkled soul
reveals that the force is still strong in her?

The Mother

Struggles with the huge child swinging
in the J of her arm – she could have put him down
with her bulging bags of formula and ingredients
for tonight's dinner –

"It's my husband's favorite" she bragged
to friends who, tasting it, could not see why –
but she continues with the child, begging
"Give Mommy a break!"

He shrieks, heads turn, sweat on her forehead
"What the hell are you looking at?" She wonders
if anyone has ever raised a baby before –
he pulls and tugs, the bags get loose

Someone offers a hand, "I'll get it! I'm a mother!"
The bags are snatched up with the baby, dinner
will be ready by six o'clock exactly –
her friends can't make it, "Kids, you know?"

The baby tears through the bag of groceries
like his father exploring the new girl on the fourth floor –
"I'll be a little late. How's the baby?"

"Fine, fine. Everything's fine."

Estella

all the pounding wing beats, her hovering presence, pressure
in metric tons, losing your own voice

a whirlwind sweeping across imaginary dragons, seeking out
the one false love able to divine

the place she missed, the tender flesh inherited—a stowaway
hidden in her gift of armor—

from each finger and filament blasted across the kill zone, she
gathered and fired you into being

a reckoning for romantic notions, foolish dreams, weakness
where every monster is born

you were born

a butterfly baby, like her,
impossibly frail, volatile, a new element in the atmosphere

flaming at the edges, living
in spite of the borrowed parts that made you insisting release

it confuses you, the stubborn blood
racing through muscle and bone, stitching and yarning patch by

patch, her accidental birth,
her mother's flight, wind and dust, silence after silence, a lover

who left her for dead, each never
dreaming of you, the weapon, the destroyer, the undying her.

Business Trip, San Antonio

Can't help
> gorging on The Alamo Buffet waffles
> and eggs any way you like them,
> hating Last Stand City
> and "Everything is Bigger"
> on every SUV, and "y'all"
> (creeping into my presentation voice,
> "Y'all, this new effin' widget will
> Change your *life*!").

Can't help
> giving in and giving up, getting
> lost in the elevated language of fevers
> "No, I'm not married
> (I don't care if you are...
> I don't care). Are you?"
> "Take your time, take away time –
> hours in cold jet cabins
> reading *Widget Monthly* –
> yeah, that's it... Change *my* life!"

Can't help
> But stay the course, of course
> *It's the American way* – to plod
> along the Riverwalk, conjure heroes
> holding off inevitable...
> Blackberry: "*Widget Industries*
> *downsizing. Meeting with shareholders*
> *not good. Sorry.*"
> Consider the dark green waters, release,
> a way to change *this* life.

Promotion

> Tragedy is a violence of smiles.
> *Christopher Arigo*

Lunch was the worst. *Congratulations!*
A banner adding to the others at the El Torrito
drinking Coronas like carefree twentysomethings
looking nothing like in cheap slacks, women
co-workers slapping the table after one drink
the hilarity of a story involving

Roberta's sister so-and-so and, well
You know who. Ha ha ha. Ha ha ha.
"The man of the hour!" all glasses raised
great, great joy, great, great good cheer
like pirates or Vikings contented
to the current plunder

and dreams of mutiny. "I just want to say
I could not have done it without..."
Everyone whoops, louder and louder
so sure it is he or she whose name
will hang off of the flaccid end
of the acknowledgment.

"Hey, awesome job," some face says
and he takes it, like he has all day, smiling.
Cell phone buzzing, buzzing – third time
in the last hour.
"You got it didn't you?"
"Please don't leave."

Soup or Salad

always amazed me, the blank stare
as if I had asked something more searching
but I was no Odysseus
clawing my way through shadows
to get to the hermaphrodite
I just wanted the order

it was simple – the choices were laid out,
in columns even, each color-coded
each seasoned with adjectives
tantalizing, luscious, delicious, sumptuous
and a little starburst, "You Get to Choose!"
but it was arduous, the choosing

and there were three other careers after that
each with their peculiar version
of a nineteen, twenty-three, thirty year old
casting out and losing himself
before he'd ever found himself
perplexed before a waiter.

Remains

Circling what is left –
      a carcass stripped of the features I might recall –
      What was it?
      Was it what you and I were looking for?

Drying up in the heat
      memory-fuel reaching Fahrenheits –
      We never reach when we should –
      Do we?

Just a bit of the living
      left after the massacre to feed on
      and fill ourselves with enough
      to sustain...

It isn't much
      and the taste leaves
      much to be desired –
      We desired so much... more!

Tear off our portions,
      growl a little, leave
      the haunting skeleton – ask,
      What was it?

Listening

Night outside of Vegas, a soft desert
sways in the Nevada heat and sun
sets in divine purple and orange
as a burning bush or blind sight

God—there in slivered clouds, desperate awe
of Sin City's outsider, alone and looking
to this sky for answers from above
and below the land is dry and empty

Why! Shouted. A question, a plea
cracked against desert's night—God
black against the glitz of The Strip down
the highway. Why? Again. Silence

The desert's dry floor absorbs the sweat
and frustration that drips in the heat
on the brow of the prodigal, laid
prostrate before a God that is mute

Like the kit fox and the desert brown owl
that watch in wonder at the man
screaming in the wind for God's voice
they had heard before he came.

Fragmentia

All, gathered, enjoyed the benefit of community
of lean and hold up, of famish and feed
and proximity.

Starting with the long crack, a divorce
of mother and father, of tension and try
no more – and the splinters:

Children falling away like scales
left in the hurry to get out
of the current skin

dragging behind, holding on
for proximity.

All, spread out, populate hungry spaces, finding
Pride cannot hold, Will cannot feed.

A piece dies waiting
to
return.

Via Negativa

One from the Chaos – Eros or Gaia – you are not.
Those who call you *first born* are not wrong; yet, you are not

Part of the Protogenoi, nor part of a prophetic line,
Nor do you dwell with Brahman, for Hindu you are not

What is your place in seconds, minutes, hours or all time?
What moment can we make you when moments you are not?

And space is none the better, and provides less to define
Agnostos Theos Paul claimed yours, though unknown you are not

For when you passed the cave and caused Moses' face to shine
You were not ineffable! Unknowable, absent, gone – you are not!

Yet, in my darkest hours, when I am reaching for you, Divine,
I often wonder if you are reaching back, and fear that you are not.

Pentecost

Where are you, Jesus? The Garden's on fire tonight –
blazing up the supplicating lilies, tulips, white faced
kneeling on black soil pews, praying you might
save the once-proud who even Solomon could not replace

Where are you, Jesus? The Garden is all a glow and heat –
petalled refugees gather in corners, browning at the edges, retracting
brazen wildflowers, like Jezebel, miserably retreat
and seek sanctuary. *Is* Your mercy everlasting?

Where are you, Jesus? The Garden's smoldering and gray –
are these Sodom's citizens: juniper carcasses, black as coal
their waxy berry eyes wonder at Your delay
and every ashen blossom begins to give up its soul.

Where are you, Jesus? The Garden's under attack again
steam rises from the lilies, all but mud remains –
I never found you, Jesus, not since the fire began.
Was a miracle too much? All I get is rain.

The Scientist

How unsatisfying for you now to watch fireworks
and know something about gun powder
or to work your tongue into another mouth
and know that no amount of rubbing
                    will start a flame.

How empty it feels now to see the sun
and know something about astronomy
or clasp onto smooth, taught thighs
and know that no amount of pulling
                    will bring down the stars.

Yet, for every wonder that you smother
with a study or a chart
and every lover that you murder
(murder that you love) no amount of failure
                    will stop a heart.

To Grow

Aren't we enlarged by the scale of
what we're able to desire?
                    Mark Doty

Holding this crystallized point of view
        and a cigarette in your flat, smileless face—
        smoke rising like the knowing airs, plain air
        from which a thousand confounding words
                are plucked before a sip
                of the coffee that makes you wise—

You can show me, in black and white, without a doubt—
        simplicity that it is—mathematical dissection of *life*—
        a word, to you, so void of mystery, banal, worthless.
        Your eyes roll with the pressure of knowing—
        and there is not world enough to impress or wake
                save the brow of scrutiny (or fear)

Of doe-eyed dreamers and life-worshippers
        passing under your grim gaze, dismissed. Life,
        the unsimple, unmeasurable word
        wrapped in wonder (by *them*), so doubted
                as if doubt were possible...
                and, perhaps, you think (like *them*) it is...

No. The Oracle of the corner café doubts
        nothing, knows everything, smokes
        and rises above the Life seekers, doubting
                as if it were possible,

As if proving anything only unproved
        everything, as if knowing were not...
        And they grow immense in doubt
        and in wonder and in hope—they grow
                because (for *them*) it is possible.

The Parable of the Tiger

for Joseph

> *What is the kingdom of God like? What*
> *shall I compare it to?*

I.

It is the hottest piece of day.
All morning we watched the chimpanzee
Because he reminded us of us
And the python who frightened
Us and made me feel lonely
With his remembering-glass eyes, steady
On our meat and soul.

It is the hour when my body
And comprehension give in.
The beasts pace behind the words,
More aware of purpose, of being
Than of the limitations, the glass
We tap at to get their gaze.
We are looking for the lion.
He is completely surrounded.

> *For many will come in my name, claiming*
> *"I am he"*

II.

You suggest we go to the elephants
To see the wisdom of their dinosaur skins
And tusks pointing to enlightenment—
Or, you say, we can watch the hawk
Trained to fly just so high
And come back down to be fed—but
We came to see the lion, I say

So we make our way to the Big Cats
And you try to tell me about the tiger—

That there is only one here—
But we both stop to take in the lion,
Alone now that the crowd has taken a picture
And tapped so long at his glass

That they've smeared
His gold and tawny glory.

> *If you, even you, had only known on this day*
> *what would bring you peace...*

III.
      His noble mane is like a wheat field, rolling.
His yawn reveals the terrible jaw, smooth
Velvet tongue in a wave, and his throat
Where a roar sleeps somewhere inside.
I catch my breath. I hear a voice.
I ask you if you hear it, too, but the lion

      And you have connected and speak
By your eyes and your careful fingers
Tracing the smudged glass wall. Again, the voice
Calls me to the far, dark, shut off cave
Where, instead of glass, a band of water
Keeps the creature and me
On opposite sides...

> *Whoever tries to keep his life will lose it, and*
> *whoever loses his life will preserve it.*

IV.
      He is like a fire in the lush green grass and bush.
His honey eyes are sweet with understanding
And I think of Blake and of you, my brother,
And I call, "Tiger, tiger..."
He leaps over the water, an urgent flame
Come like a hungry rapture.

V.

       Where is the tiger? I ask, weary,
Half dead in my broken body I just
Now noticed to be broken—
It almost killed you, you say, so they
Locked him away... far away.
Tell me they didn't kill it, I say with tears.

No, you tell me, he's the only one
we have, brother.

This Life More Sweet

The alternative:
Ending in the bottle,
ending just before the ending
and forgetting
the number of drinks, the number of years,
the point
and washing away your shadow.

The alternative:
Melting away in a moment
when just a little resilience, even a step or two
away from the flame, away from the moment
might have saved us all
the trouble of scraping you up
from the bottom of our cares.

There are endings all around,
pacing the sidewalks and malls without a shadow
or a thought as to
where they might have gone.

And there are moments
who hunt us like oxygen
and crave to consume not only us
but every molecule
we connected to.

And the alternative:
endure.

Acknowledgements

Profound gratitude to the following publications and their editors for finding a place for my words. The poems listed below may have been altered since their original publications:

Cadence Collective: "In the Ball Crawl." "Dumbo the Flying Elephant." "Projects Prayer." "Sons of Thunder." "We Were the Tide." "Something Significant."
Coldnoon: Travel Poetics: "Listening." "Business Trip, San Antonio." "Rijksmuseum, 2012."
Dash Literary Journal: "Stars." (as "Such Sweet Things")
Dual Coast Magazine: "Pitfalls." "Son of a Bitch." "Faraway Words on Jars." "Filipino Food."
Eunoia Review: "The Vertical View of History Holds." "Contiguous We."
Indiana University Northwest's Spirits Magazine: "The Far Reaches of What Humans Can Find." "I Would." "Soup or Salad."
Kansas State University's Touchstone Magazine: "This Life More Sweet." "You Gonna Be Up All Night." "Buttercream."
Loch Raven Review: "The Home."
Mused: The Bella Online Literary Journal: "The Mother."
Poetry Quarterly: "Jingle Bells & Jazz." "Taking It In."
San Pedro River Review: "Deluge."
Scholars & Rogues: "Wonderland."
The Copperfield Review: "Fragmentia." "Remains."
The Louisville Review: "Chow Hall."
The Thirty First Bird Review: "Via Negativa."
Trailer Park Quarterly: "Promotion."
Wilde Magazine: "On the Dance Floor."
Zingara Poetry Picks: "Like Her."

Gratitude

Thank you, Sarah (Tatro) Thursday, for taking on my vision and for breathing life into the Long Beach poetry community. Thank you, Josephine Durkin, for granting me the privilege to feature your work on the cover. Thanks also to my many mentors, especially Irena Praitis and Frank X. Gaspar who taught me to write (and live) with great love and great hope. I am indebted to the poets, colleagues, students, friends, and family who have inspired and supported me. My boys, Craig, Marcus, William, and Philip; my Disneyland/Plaid family; my Texas family, Sean, Allyson, Erin, Vince, and the Ferrier-Watsons; my Cal State Fullerton and Texas A&M University-Commerce families; and especially my blood, the Isips, the Flynns, the Merediths and their endless array of progeny—I love you.

To you, Reader, *Thank you.* I know you didn't have to; I hope it was worth it.

About the Author

J.D. Isip is a Professor of English at Collin College in Plano, Texas and the Editor of the online literary journal, *Ishaan Literary Review.* His poetry, plays, short fiction, and academic works have appeared in several print and online journals and reviews. In addition, J.D. has published a composition textbook with Fountainhead Press, *This is Writing: A Conceptual Guide to College Writing.* This is his first full-length poetry collection.

Find Out More

You can read poems by J.D. and other poets from Long Beach, California (where J.D. spent most of his life) at **CadenceCollective.net** Check out J.D.'s work as an Editor at **IshaanLiteraryReview.com** You can follow J.D. on Twitter **@ProfJDIsip**

The fantastic artwork for the cover comes from Josephine Durkin. You can find out more about her and her work at: **JosephineDurkin.com**

About the Cover Art

The background detail and the individual art piece featured on the cover come from Josephine Durkin's *Gathering Flora* collection. Each piece is composed of sewn digital prints on photo rag, Color-Aid paper, latex, acrylic and pastel on paper.

Photographs:
The photos on the back cover are of Margaret Mangahas, J.D.'s mother, and a high school photo of J.D. and his friend, W. Cody Wilson.

Notes for "Hundreds of Smaller Deaths"

[1] Sheol is an Old Testament term for "pit" or "abyss."

[2] Paul watched the disciple Stephen get stoned; Stephen famously says, "I see heaven" which paints the picture that he sees what the unbelieving do not see, including Paul (who will be struck blind shortly after this)

[3] Emily Dickinson, "I shall know why – when Time is over - " (215)

[4] Shakespeare's Lady Macbeth from *Macbeth*

[5] Pilate washes his hands in a bowl before the crowd crying for Jesus to be crucified

[6] W.H. Auden "As I Walked Out One Evening"

[7] Shakespeare's *Julius Caesar III.ii.147-8*

[8] Jorges Luis Borges, "Luke XXIII" trans:

> Death by crucifixion,
> He learned from the taunts of the crowd
> That the man who was dying beside him
> Was God.

[9] Paul is beheaded like John the Baptist (whose head was served on a silver platter to Salome, according to legend)

[10] Marlowe's *Edward the Second XXV.74*

[11] Shakespeare's *King Lear IV.vi.150-51*

[12] Daniel 5:20 trans from French: "But when his heart was lifted up and his spirit became so proud that he behaved arrogantly, he was deposed from his royal throne and his glory was taken away from him."

[13] Ralph Waldo Emerson, *The Poet*

[14] "O" conflates by Ovid and Omega, here the tale of Midas and Jesus' explanation of signs of the times

[15] John Greenleaf Whittier "Snow Bound"

[16] This and two lines above from Phyllis Wheatley "On Being Brought from Africa to America"

[17] Marianne Moore "He 'Digesteth Harde Yron'"

[18] This and two lines above from Marianne Moore "What Are Years?"

[19] Ben Jonson *Epicene IV.i.20-21*

[20] Acts 20:24

[21] From "Tu Vuò Fa l'Americano" by Renato Carosone.
Translated:

How can your loved one understand
If you're speaking half American?
When you're out loving under the moon,
Where do you get a phrase like "I love you"?

[22] Theodore Roethke "My Papa's Waltz"

[23] 2 Timothy 2:1

[24] Paul's good friend/lover. Stephen Schwartz "Einmal" from the musical *Der Glöckner von Notre Dame* runs through whole poem.

[25] Deuteronomy 6:6-7 trans from Italian: "These words, which I am commanding you today, shall be on your heart. You shall teach them diligently to your sons and shall talk of them when you sit in your house and when you walk by the way and when you lie down and when you rise up."

[26] This and following right side of music, from Psalm 8

[27] *I used to believe*
In the days I was naive
That I'd live to see
A day of justice dawn
And though I will die
Long before that morning comes
I'll die while believing still
It will come when I am gone

[28] Greek for Antioch

[29] Barnabas

[30] (Chorus)
Someday
When we are wiser
When the world's older
When we have learned
I pray
Someday we may yet live
To live and let live

[31] Robert Hayden "Those Winter Sundays"

[32] *Someday*
Life will be fairer

Need will be rarer
Greed will not pay
God speed
This bright millennium
On its way
Let it come someday

[33] Frances Ellen Watkins Harper "The Slave Auction"

[34] Jack Kerouac "Heaven"

[35] *There are some days*
Black and bitter
It seems we haven't got a prayer

[36] John Dryden *Absalom and Achitophel,* lines 985-88

[37] *But a prayer for something better*

[38] Pound's "A Pact"

[39] *Is the one thing we all share*

[40] Rudyard Kipling "Epitaphs of War"

[41] *We all share...*
Someday
Our fight will be one then
We'll stand in the sun then
That bright afternoon
Till then
On days when the sun is gone
Hope lives on
Wish upon the moon
Change will come

[42] 1 Corinthians 13:1-3

[43] Paraphrase from Henry Rollins "I Know You"

[44] Verse from Pound's *A Lume Spento* carried over to his *Personae* introduction

[45] Euripides *Medea,* lines 1222-4

[46] Sophocles *Oedipus the King,* lines 781-2

[47] Aeschylus *Agamemnon,* lines 1295-7 (altered slightly to sound like both Paul and Cassandra)

[48] Dante *The Divine Comedy, Inferno, Canto III, lines 30-31*

[49] From songwriter Matt Nathanson

[50] Vague reference to Proust's *Remembrance of Things Past*

[51] William Carlos Williams "Asphodel, That Greeny Flower"

[52] Louvre Museum, Paris

[53] Philip II

[54] Greek, "To the Unknown God"

[55] Acts 17:23

[56] Henry Wadsworth Longfellow "A Psalm to Life"

[57] Paraphrase from Ranier Maria Rilke's *Letters to a Young Poet*

[58] Romans 16:17

[59] Bertolt Brecht "The Dying Poet's Address to Young People"

[60] Michelangelo, Sonnet 151

[61] Elizabeth Bishop "Filling Station"

[62] Loose reference to Deleuze and Guattari's *Capitalism and Schizophrenia*

[63] John 1:1 "In the beginning was the Word, and the Word was with God, and the Word was God." (Chinese Union Version)

[64] Confucius, *Analects*, Book II, 21

[65] Aristotle, *Poetics*

[66] Cleanth Brooks, "The Formalist Critics"

[67] Ferdinand de Saussure, "Course in General Linguistics"

[68] Deleuze and Guattari, "The Anti-Oedipus"

[69] Luce Irigaray, "Commodities amongst Themselves"

[70] Slightly altered from Edward Said's "Orientalism"

[71] 1 Timothy 1:15

[72] *Lancelot of the Laik*, lines 3365-66

[73] Thomas Kyd, *The Spanish Tragedy*, III.ii.10-11

[74] Siegfried Sassoon, "On Passing the New Menin Gate"

[75] Legend of Fergus mac Róich: One day, after Fergus has been in exile for fourteen years, Ailill sees him swimming in a lake with Medb, and is overcome with jealousy. He tells his brother, Lugaid Dalleces, who is blind, that deer are playing in the water, and persuades him to throw a spear at them. He does so, and the spear hits Fergus in the chest.

[76] Brian Turner, "Here, Bullet"

[77] Shakespeare's *I Henry IV*, I.ii.180-82

[78] C.P. Cavafy, "The Horses of Achilles"

[79] Pound from *Canto LXXVIII*

[80] Aftermath of Paul's letter to the Romans about homosexuality, a link to the last line of "Mamertinum: Timothy" when Paul says, "How could I know I would penetrate the future?"

[81] Lord Alfred Douglas – Paul begins by talking about Oscar Wilde

[82] E.M. Forster *Maurice*

[83] This and following in italics, Pound's "Picadilly"

[84] Paul Monette "Half Life"

[85] Tom Stoppard *The Invention of Love*

[86] A.E. Houseman "He would not stay for me, and who can wonder"

[87] Lifted from my poem, "Stars"

[88] Ezra Pound (EP) *Canto LXXX*, lines 661-62

[89] Walt Whitman, "To a Common Prostitute"

[90] EP *Canto LXXXI*, line 55, "To break the pentameter, that was the first heave" altered to fit Paul with the "thorn" which some attribute to homosexual desire

[91] 1 Samuel 18:3-4

[92] 1 Samuel 20:4

[93] Philippians 4:8

[94] EP *Canto LXXXIII*, line235

[95] Story by Raymond Carver

[96] From my poem, "I Would"

[97] *Darest Thou Now O Soul* Walt Whitman

[98] The name of the bar where Matthew Shepard met his murderers

[99] At the eulogy of Matthew Shepard, his father, Dennis, said that he and his son would go out and look at the stars at night, that it would be one of the things he would miss most.

[100] *Sometimes With One I Love* Walt Whitman

[101] Aaron James McKinney: along with Russell Arthur Henderson, lured Matthew Shepard out of the Fireside Lounge, claiming to be gay. The two men pistol whipped Shepard and took him into an empty field where they beat him until he was unconscious and tied him to a deer fence, where he was discovered by a bicyclist who thought he was a scarecrow.

[102] *A Sight in Camp in the Daybreak Gray and Dim* Walt Whitman

[103] *Look Down Fair Moon* Walt Whitman

[104] *The Sleepers* Walt Whitman

[105] Aaron, in *The Exodus*, responds to the desperate Israelites by creating a golden calf for them to worship in the desert while they waited for Moses to return from Sinai

[106] The night Matthew Shepard was pronounced dead, massive protests/vigils sprung up across the nation, with crowds in the thousands in New York and San Francisco

[107] *O Tan-Faced Prairie Boy* Walt Whitman

[108] *O Me! O Life!* Walt Whitman

Made in the USA
San Bernardino, CA
17 October 2015